Cooking Well

Healthy Italian

OVER 100 EASY & DELICIOUS RECIPES

Lauryn Colatuno, Mary Ann Colatuno
and Cecilia Pappano with Jo Brielyn

))) hatherleigh

Hatherleigh Press is committed to preserving and protecting the natural resources of the earth. Environmentally responsible and sustainable practices are embraced within the company's mission statement.

Visit us at www.hatherleighpress.com and register online for free offers, discounts, special events, and more.

Cooking Well: Healthy Italian

DISCLAIMER
This book offers general cooking and eating suggestions for educational purposes only. In no case should it be a substitute nor replace a healthcare professional. Consult your healthcare professional to determine which foods are safe for you and to establish the right diet for your personal nutritional needs.

Library of Congress Cataloging-in-Publication Data is available upon request.

ISBN 978-1-57826-482-7

All Hatherleigh Press titles are available for bulk purchase, special promotions, and premiums. For information about reselling and special purchase opportunities, please call 1-800-528-2550 and ask for the Special Sales Manager.

Cover and Interior Design by Nick Macagnone
Photos on pages 35, 75, and 145 by Porto Bay Events used under the Creative Commons Attribution License 2.0.
Photo on page 130 used under the Creative Commons Attribution License 2.0.

10 9 8 7 6 5 4 3 2
Printed in the United States

Table of Contents

CHAPTER 1

The History of Italian Cuisine

The delicious taste of Italian cuisine has become one of the most popular food choices for people all over the world, and it's easy to see why. With so many clever and easy-to-prepare combinations of zesty sauces, garden vegetables, delectable cheeses, and fresh meat and seafood, Italian cuisine contains some of the most varied and satisfying dishes in the world. The delightful tastes, coupled with the simplicity of ingredients that Italian dishes are known for, are what make Italian cuisine an extremely appealing option in many homes. Italian cuisine promotes simple cooking, concentrating on unique flavors as well as the appearance and texture of each ingredient used. Olive oil is not simply oil. Garlic, tomatoes, and vegetables must be fresh. Traditional Italian recipes illustrate that creating healthy and mouthwatering dishes is all about the *quality* of the ingredients you use, not the *quantity* of them.

Even the mere mention of Italian food is enough to conjure up images of heavy, fattening pasta dishes, loaded with meat, cheeses, and thick tomato- or cream-based sauces. But the truth is that, while many Italian restaurants in the United States serve this sort of fare to their customers, this is not typical of the traditional cuisine found in Italy.

In order to better understand the eclectic origin and makeup of traditional Italian cuisine, it will be helpful to know a little background of the history of Italy itself. Although Italy is still fairly young as a country (at just over 150 years old), the region itself is very old. Prior to becoming its own country, the region of Italy was sectioned into kingdoms, princedoms, dukedoms, republics, and papal areas. The inhabitants of those separate areas had little contact with one another, so recipes and ingredients were not shared among the people.

The varying climate and geographical differences among the regions in Italy have impacted the ingredient choices as well. The Italian people of each region gravitate toward the foods that are in season and readily available to them for everyday cooking. In the northern plains of Italy, pastures and cows are plentiful, so beef and veal are the staple meats found in northern-inspired dishes. Of course, where there are plentiful dairy cows, ingredients such as milk, butter, and cream are readily available and frequently incorporated into foods. Dishes prepared in the mountainous regions of southern Italy, by contrast, have goat, lamb, pork, and chicken as the main meat sources. Pecorino cheese, which is made from sheep's milk, is also used more often.

Italian cooking has also been affected by the cuisines of several cultures, such as those of the Etruscan, Greek, Roman, Moorish, and Arabic civilizations. Before Italy became its own nation, it was ruled and inhabited by a variety of empires, the influences of which are evident in everything from architecture to the history of Italian food. Drawing on culinary influences from such varied sources, Italian cuisine had evolved many times over before becoming the popular dishes that we know and appreciate today.

Here are a few of the influential cultures that have contributed to the development and transformation of Italian cuisine throughout the centuries.

Etruscans: The most important contribution the Etruscans made to Italian cuisine was *pulmentum*. Pulmentum is a mushy, grain-based dish that is in essence a type of porridge. It originally served as a predecessor to polenta, which is a cornmeal-based porridge that is popular throughout Italy.

Greeks: The Greek nation introduced fish chowder to Italy (called *bouillabaisse* in France and *brodetto* in southern Italy).

Romans: During the time when Rome maintained control of Italy, the Roman Empire introduced exotic ingredients and spices such as ginger, pepper, and salt to the inhabitants of the Italian peninsula.

Moors: The use of couscous, citrus fruits, and almonds in recipes were introduced into Italian cuisine by the Moors.

Arabs: The dried pasta widely used in Italy and most Italian cuisine today actually originated with the Arabic population, which was especially influential in Sicily and the southern parts of the Italian mainland.

Italian Cuisine from Region to Region

Traditional Italian cuisine varies widely from region to region. Italy is comprised of 20 regions, each with their own distinct characteristics. In towns and villages across the country, Italians create the same dishes, each with its own variation or flair to mark it as distinct to that region. Each region generally also has a dish that is its prized specialty. Below are a few of the regions in Italy and the foods most often associated with them.

Tuscany

Recipes for the region of Tuscany generally have a blend of vegetables, white beans, saltless bread, and fruity olive oil. Popular spices in Tuscan recipes are thyme, rosemary, and fennel. They also use sharp, salty cheeses from sheep's milk to flavor their pastas, salads, and savory pies. Tuscan dishes, like their famous hearty soups, often include rice or risotto. Ravioli and tortelli filled with ricotta cheese are premier among the region's classic stuffed pastas.

Sicily

Sicily, the largest island in the Mediterranean, is the home of *gelato* (Italian ice cream) and many desserts made with Marsala wine. Sicilian cuisine draws a lot of influence from Arabic cuisine, so its recipes, especially pastries, often include citrus fruits, almonds, and pistachios. Cooks in Sicily have a penchant for blending sweet and sour flavors in their foods. For example, *caponata*, a Sicilian favorite, is made of eggplants fried and flavored with vinegar and sugar. The region is also known for its fish stews and vegetables.

Abruzzo

Pork, sheep, and goat are the main meats eaten in Abruzzo, since the region is predominantly a mountainous area where livestock is raised. Cuisine in this region differs from most Italian food because it includes hot peppers such as peperoncinos and red chili peppers called *diavolinos* or "little devils." Abruzzo is the most prominent producer of saffron in Italy, and its unique flavor is used in many local dishes.

Veneto

The region of Veneto is known for its tasty soups and risottos with seafood and sausage. Pasta is far less popular in this area. Instead, cooks use polenta, gnocchi, and rice (risotto) for their dishes. The famous *pasta e fagioli* is one of the few dishes from the Veneto region that actually uses pasta.

Campania

The region of Campania is the homeland of pizza. It is also famous for excellent tomato sauces, mozzarella, and pasta dishes. Shellfish pasta, fish stews, and meat sauces flavored with garlic, herbs, and tomatoes are also common. This region is also known for its cakelike, ricotta-filled pastries known as *sfogliatelle* and liqueur-soaked yeast buns called *babà*.

Emilia-Romagna

Emilia-Romagna—one of the larger regions in northern Italy—boasts a rich, refined culture of food and wine, all centered on its capital of Bologna, the culinary center of the nation. While much of Italian cuisine draws on the fresh seafood available on the Adriatic coast, Emilia-Romagna is more famous for its meat dishes, especially those using pork. Many of the most famous dishes in Italian cuisine are perfected in Bolognese kitchens, including such pasta dishes as tortellini, lasagna, and tagliatelle, as well as Bolognese meat sauce, mortedella, gnocchi, and so much more.

CHAPTER 2

The Staples of Italian Cuisine and Their Health Benefits

I talian cuisine, prepared using healthy methods and fresh ingredients, is exemplary of the Mediterranean style of eating: it focuses on simple, natural ingredients such as tomatoes, garlic, olive oil, dark leafy greens, and whole grains. Most Italian meals balance carbohydrates with proteins, as well as include a variety of fresh fruits and vegetables. Creating healthy Italian cuisine starts with purchasing the freshest ingredients possible. When you use fresh, high-quality ingredients, you don't have to overload your dish with fat and salt.

The food items listed on the next few pages include just a few of the staple ingredients found in Italian cuisine and the nutritional benefits that each offers.

Olive Oil

Olive oil is a healthy choice to use for cooking and is included in a variety of Mediterranean recipes. It contains the healthy monounsaturated fats that benefit your body. Monounsaturated fats help reduce cholesterol levels and lower your risk of heart disease. They also give your body high amounts of vitamin E, which is important for maintaining the immune system.

Storage Tip for Keeping Olive Oil Fresh: Heat and light are the worst enemies of maintaining the quality of olive oil, so do not use clear bottles and avoid keeping bottles in places that will receive direct sunlight. Instead, always store olive oil in a cool, dark cupboard.

Common Grades of Olive Oil

Unlike most other cooking oils, olive oil comes in a variety of grades, each with a slightly different flavor. Here are the common grades of olive oil.

Extra Virgin Olive Oil: Extra virgin olive oil is considered to be the premium grade and is made from the first pressing of olives. The oil is extracted using a cold pressing method that involves no chemicals and requires only a small amount of heat during the process.

Virgin Olive Oil: Virgin olive oil is made from the second pressing of olives. It is extracted using the same cold pressing method used for extra virgin olive oil: again, no chemicals and only minimal heat are involved.

Non-Virgin Olive Oil: Non-virgin oil is commercial-grade olive oil. While it is usually marketed as "pure" olive oil, this is true only to the extent that the only ingredient in it is olive oil. It is, however, made from the remains of lower-quality olives *after* they have been pressed repeatedly to extract the virgin oil. Non-virgin olive oil goes through a process that involves chemicals, heat, high pressure, and filtration to refine it. Oftentimes, non-virgin olive oil is mixed with a small amount of virgin olive oil to renew the natural color and flavor before it is marketed. Non-virgin olive oil is the grade of olive oil most often bought by people for everyday use.

Light and Extra Light Olive Oil: Light and extra light olive oil are created from the last pressings of olives. They are of a lower quality and are more refined than the other grades. They also offer far fewer health benefits. Light and extra light olive oils do not possess much natural olive flavor or color. They are often used as a substitute in baking to replace butter specifically because the olive flavor is less pronounced.

Tomatoes

Tomatoes contain lycopene, an antioxidant that is known to fight heart disease, cancer, high cholesterol, and a variety of other illnesses. They also provide your body with high quantities of fiber, potassium, and vitamins A, C, and K.

Did You Know?

Tomatoes were not a staple in traditional Italian cuisine until they were introduced into Europe in the sixteenth century. Before tomatoes were incorporated into Italian cooking, most Italian cooks had prepared dishes using staples like olive oil, garlic, fish, flatbread, game meat, cheeses, and seasonal fruits and vegetables. But now tomatoes, cheese, and pasta make up the base for the majority of Italian meals.

Garlic

Garlic has been a popular ingredient in Italian cuisine for centuries. Not only does garlic add flavor to dishes, it also kills bacteria, prevents diarrhea, and aids in digestion. Garlic has also been linked to reducing the risks of colon and stomach cancer.

Did You Know?

The beneficial sulfide minerals found in garlic are not released unless the garlic is crushed or chopped and allowed to sit for at least 10 to 15 minutes. Make sure to account for this time before eating it or using it in your cooking. Garlic bought in the store that is already chopped offers the same benefits.

Seafood

Seafood is a key source of protein in Italian cuisine. This is due largely to the fact that almost any location in Italy is 100 miles or less from the water, so fresh fish and seafood are readily accessible in markets. All varieties of shellfish and fish are used. Commonly used types of seafood are shrimp, scallops, crab, mussels, clams, squid, tuna, anchovies, sardines, cod, salmon, and sea bass. Often there will be several different types of seafood used in the same dish. In addition to protein, seafood also offers benefits such as potassium, omega-3 fatty acids, calcium, niacin, selenium, and vitamins B and D.

Whole Grains

Whole grains (or unrefined grains) such as whole wheat pasta, whole grain breads, semolina, barley, and whole wheat couscous are staples in Italian cuisine. Grains left in their whole form have a lower glycemic index, so they are digested more slowly. Whole grains also keep all of their fiber, magnesium, and vitamin E benefits, which are significantly reduced by the refinement process used for white breads and pastas. Beneficial nutrients found in whole grains also help fight against heart disease, diabetes, and other chronic diseases.

Cheese

Cheese is a central ingredient in Italian cuisine. Some cheeses are simply sliced and eaten fresh; others are blended with herbs to create pasta dishes. Many of the cheeses are dried and shaved or sprinkled over Italian dishes to complete them. Cheeses are also used to create delectable Italian desserts. Cheeses offer a variety of nutrients to the body, such as calcium, zinc, and vitamins A and D. Some of the common cheeses included in Italian cuisine are mozzarella, Parmigiano-Reggiano, Asiago, gorgonzola, pecorino, provolone, and ricotta.

Beans

Beans are grown throughout Italy and are therefore commonly included in a variety of traditional Italian recipes. Often they are used to replace meat, while still providing the necessary protein. Beans and other legumes like chickpeas and lentils are popular choices. Beans offer beneficial nutrients such as fiber, iron, magnesium, copper, calcium, folic acid, and zinc. Beans are also believed to reduce the risk of heart disease, help manage diabetes, and prevent colon cancer.

White beans are popular in Italian cuisine. Some of the most commonly used are cannellini (white kidney beans that are also referred to as *fagioli*), soranini, toscanello, corona, and schiaccioni. Other types of beans found in Italian dishes include lentils, fava beans, and borlotti beans.

Nuts

Nut trees are almost as common as olive trees in Italy, and nuts receive a similarly frequent amount of use in recipes. Whether eaten fresh as a snack, added to salads, chopped for baked goods, or ground for use in sauces or pestos, nuts have their place throughout Italian cuisine. Nuts are packed with good monounsaturated fat, fiber, protein, folic acid, calcium, magnesium, and vitamins B and E. Popular nuts used in Italian cuisine are almonds, walnuts, and pine *(pignoli)* nuts.

Dark Leafy Greens

Italian recipes also include generous portions of rich, dark leafy greens such as chard, kale, escarole, and collards. These foods offer excellent nutritional benefits such as magnesium, potassium, and vitamins A, B, C, E, and K.

Emmer

Emmer, or *farro* as it is traditionally called in Italy, is an ancient variety of grain known to be among the first grains domesticated in the Near East. Popularized and spread by the Romans, emmer is now grown almost exclusively in select regions of Italy. Often used to create hearty breads, it has also grown in popularity as a whole grain used in Tuscan soups. Possessing a higher fiber content than common wheat, its health benefits have led many to develop emmer pasta as a healthier alternative to wheat pasta. If you are looking to add emmer to your diet, try the recipes on pages 55 and 93.

CHAPTER 3

Cooking and Dining Tips

The recipes included in *Cooking Well: Healthy Italian* are prepared in accordance with the mindset that the healthier way to cook and eat is to use a smaller amount of real, flavorful ingredients rather than substituting with lower-calorie, artificial products. A little butter and olive oil go a long way in adding flavor and satisfying the desire for good food. The addition of homemade broths to many recipes can help to reduce the fat content and add a burst of fresh, natural flavor.

Simplicity is the key to creating Italian recipes that are delicious and healthy. Adding too many ingredients can cause them to overpower each other and confuse the taste buds until it's impossible to even determine what you are supposed to be tasting. Instead, rely on fresh and in-season items to provide the flavor to your recipes. Try to get vegetables and fruits from your own garden, the local farmers' market, or a farm co-op so you are able to use the freshest and most healthful ingredients.

Experimentation with different fresh herbs and other natural flavoring ingredients such as honey is strongly encouraged. Natural herbs and seasonings add so much additional flavor to healthier versions of Italian dishes that the elimination of extra salt or fat will not even be detected in the taste of the final products.

Simple Tips for Preparing Healthy Italian Cuisine

- Blend fresh parsley and basil with high-quality olive oil and vinegars in a food processor to create a creamy salad dressing instead of using mayonnaise or cream-based dressings.

- Add a teaspoon of Dijon mustard and a dollop of honey to the salad dressing above, and you have yet another fresh, unique salad dressing that is healthy and bursting with flavor.

- Make batches of fresh tomato sauce when the tomatoes are sweet and in season, and freeze the marinara sauce to use as needed.

- Consider lemon as a go-to flavor to spark up your recipes. Just a few squirts of fresh lemon juice adds a special zing to a variety of foods from salad dressings to gravies to pasta dishes.

- Try substituting with whole grain and whole wheat pastas in recipes. There are good-quality versions that have a nice flavor while still providing you with the benefits of whole grains.

- Meat substitutions can also be made to create healthier versions of recipes. Lean cuts of meat can replace fattier meats in recipes without losing too much taste, especially when the dish is seasoned correctly. Turkey or chicken can often be used in place of beef and pork in many recipes too.

- Buy extra small grape or cherry tomatoes when they are in season and prepare them for later use. Slow roast with olive oil, a dash of salt, and minced garlic, and then freeze them to use in meals later when they are no longer in season. The same procedure can be used to roast red peppers as well.

- If you make your own stock or broth, freeze it in plastic bags or containers for more convenient use for future recipes. For individual-size portions, try pouring small amounts into ice cube trays and storing them in the freezer.

Keeping Your Italian Choices Healthy

Whether you are preparing your favorite Italian dishes at home or dining out, it is possible to find healthy alternatives. Here are a few ways to enjoy tasty choices without sacrificing your healthy goals.

- Choose meals that are grilled, roasted, sautéed, or baked, not fried.

- Focus on dishes that make vegetables or seafood the main ingredients. Recipes that use chicken and lean cuts of beef and pork are also good choices to have on occasion.

- Replace refined grains with whole grain options. When eating out, try to select menu items that use whole grain pastas and breads or ask the waiter if it is possible to substitute with them.

- Cut down on how much you eat of the more fattening Italian food items by beginning your meal with a healthy soup and/or salad choice. Also limit your bread intake.

- Stay away from the thick, cream-based sauces and opt for ones that are broth- or tomato-based instead.

CHAPTER 4

The Recipes

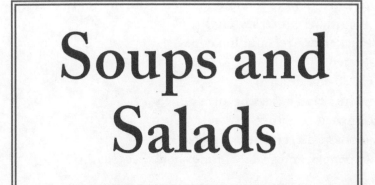

Soups and Salads

Economical Vegetable Soup

Serves 6

Ingredients

Any frozen vegetables you may have on hand in your freezer
(such as corn, peas, carrots, etc.)
3 or 4 chicken or beef bouillon cubes
4 cups water
1 can chickpeas, drained
1 can white or red kidney beans, drained
½ cup crushed tomatoes
2 teaspoons garlic, crushed
Sea salt, pepper, and grated Parmesan cheese (to taste)

Directions

Place frozen vegetables and bouillon cubes in water in 4-quart pot.
Cook until tender. Add chickpeas, kidney beans, tomatoes, and seasonings. Simmer for 1 hour. Serve hot.

Garlic Soup

Serves 4

Ingredients

2 bulbs garlic
2 tablespoons olive oil
1 tablespoon olive oil, whipped
butter, or light butter
6 cloves garlic, peeled and
chopped
1 medium red onion, chopped
1 (32 oz.) container chicken
broth (preferably organic)

2 tablespoons half-and-half (you
can substitute with fat-free half-
and-half)
2 tablespoons shaved Locatelli
Romano cheese
1 lemon
Sea salt and pepper (to taste)

Directions

Cut off top of two garlic bulbs, place on foil, and drizzle 1
tablespoon of olive oil and just a sprinkle of sea salt on the garlic
bulbs. Wrap in the foil and bake at 350°F for about 30 minutes.

While the garlic is roasting, melt the butter and remaining
tablespoon of olive oil in a saucepan. Add the chopped garlic and
onions and sauté until soft. Squeeze the baked garlic into the same
saucepan. Add the chicken broth and simmer for about 15 minutes
on low heat. Add the cream and cool. Put soup through blender
until smooth. Reheat on low, and squeeze in the juice of one lemon.
Serve with shaved Romano cheese.

Healthy Lentil Soup

Serves 8

Ingredients

½ pound turkey sausage
1 cup lentils, rinsed
2 cups low-sodium chicken broth
5 cups water
4 fresh carrots, sliced and chopped
1 white onion, chopped
2 teaspoons chopped garlic
2 tablespoons olive oil
¼ cup fresh, chopped parsley
Grated Romano cheese (to taste)
Sea salt and pepper (to taste)

Directions

Remove sausage from casing, crumble, and brown in a nonstick pan for 10 minutes. Drain sausage, and add lentils and broth to the water in a Dutch oven. Cook lentils until tender. Add carrots, onion, garlic, olive oil, turkey, and seasonings. Simmer for 1 hour, and serve with grated cheese.

Note: You may find it necessary to add more water since the lentils will absorb the liquid. You may also prefer to delete sausage if you wish it to be meatless.

Italian Wedding Soup

Serves 8

Ingredients

1 egg
¾ pound lean ground turkey
½ cup chopped onion
2 tablespoons chopped fresh parsley
¼ Italian seasoned breadcrumbs
4 tablespoons grated Romano cheese
8 cups low-sodium chicken broth

4 large carrots, chopped
2 stalks celery, chopped
1¼ cups acini di pepe pasta
Sea salt, pepper, and garlic powder (to taste)

Directions

In large bowl, stir together egg, turkey, onion, parsley, breadcrumbs, 2 tablespoons of cheese, salt, pepper, and garlic powder. Form into 1-inch balls and place on a baking sheet. Refrigerate while preparing the rest of the soup. Combine broth, carrots, and celery in a stockpot. Add turkey meatballs. Cover and cook on low for 3 hours. Stir in pasta for the last 20 minutes. Add additional salt and pepper to taste. Sprinkle each serving with Romano cheese.

Minestrone

Serves 6

Ingredients

2 tablespoons olive oil
1 large onion, diced
4 cloves garlic, minced
1 teaspoon dried oregano
1 teaspoon dried basil
1 (15 oz.) can kidney beans,
drained and rinsed
1 (15 oz.) can garbanzo beans,
drained and rinsed

1 (28 oz.) can diced tomatoes
1 (14 oz.) can crushed tomatoes
6 cups low-sodium chicken broth
1 can green beans
1 cup whole wheat bowtie pasta
Sea salt and pepper (to taste)

Directions

Heat the olive oil in a large pot over medium-high heat. Add the onion and cook until soft. Add the garlic and cook for 1 minute. Stir in the dried oregano and basil, salt, and pepper. Add the kidney beans, green beans and garbanzo beans, diced and crushed tomatoes, and the chicken broth to the pot and bring to a boil. Reduce the heat to medium and cook for 10 minutes. Stir in the pasta and simmer until the pasta and vegetables are tender.

Pasta Fagioli

Serves 6

Ingredients

2 tablespoons olive oil
5 stalks celery, chopped
1 onion, chopped
2 (48 oz.) cans low-sodium chicken broth
1 (8 oz.) can plain tomato sauce
2 cans cannellini beans
5 carrots, peeled and chopped
½ pound ditalini pasta
Sea salt, pepper, and garlic (to taste)

Directions

Pour olive oil in a large skillet. Sauté celery until tender; add onion and sauté until translucent. Season with salt, pepper, and garlic. Pour in chicken broth and tomato sauce. Add cannellini beans with the juice. Put carrots in the soup and cook on medium heat for about ½ hour. In a separate pan cook pasta according to the directions on the box. Always keep the pasta separate from the soup until each serving.

Note: If added to soup the pasta will become too soft and soak up too much juice.

Roasted Tomato Soup with Basil

Serves 4

Ingredients

3 cups fresh, chopped tomatoes
2 cloves garlic
½ teaspoon smoked paprika
Dash kosher salt
Dash ground pepper
2 tablespoons good-quality olive oil
2 cups low-sodium chicken broth
½ cup fresh basil
Juice of ½ lemon

2 tablespoons cream (you can substitute with low-fat milk or evaporated milk if you prefer, but a little cream gives it a great smooth taste)
Romano or Parmesan cheese shavings

Directions

Place chopped tomatoes, garlic, smoked paprika, salt, pepper, and olive oil in a bowl and toss. Place on a parchment-lined cookie sheet and bake at 350°F for about 20 minutes or until tomatoes are soft and beginning to brown. Place chicken broth, tomatoes, fresh basil, lemon juice, and tomato mixture in a food processor until blended and it thickens. Place in a soup pot and add cream. Top with finely shaved Romano or Parmesan cheese. This is a great soup to fix when you have tomatoes you must use quickly. Freezes great.

Baby Greens and Pear Salad

Serves 6

Ingredients

1 package baby greens or 2 cups fresh greens from garden
¼ cup olive oil
⅛ cup balsamic vinegar or favorite balsamic vinaigrette dressing
12 grape tomatoes, halved
1 can small, pitted black olives, halved
½ cup chopped walnuts
6 fresh pears, sliced (peeled or unpeeled)
¼ cup low-fat or nonfat feta cheese
Sea salt and pepper (to taste)

Directions

Mix greens with olive oil, vinegar, salt, and pepper. Place on a flat tray or dish. Arrange tomatoes, olives, walnuts, and pears on top of greens and around the edges. Sprinkle with feta cheese.

Cannellini and Asparagus Salad

Serves 4

Ingredients

½ pound small red potatoes, sliced

12 thin asparagus spears, cut into 2-inch pieces

1 (16 oz.) can cannellini beans, rinsed and drained

1 small red onion, chopped

2 tablespoons minced scallions

2 tablespoons apple juice

2 tablespoons olive oil

2 teaspoons Dijon mustard

2 teaspoons grated lemon peel

1 teaspoon red wine vinegar

Sea salt and pepper (to taste)

Directions

Place potatoes in a 3-quart saucepan. Cover with cold water and cook for 10 minutes. Add the asparagus and cook for 5 more minutes. Drain and rinse with cold water. Put into a large bowl and add beans, onions, and scallions and mix lightly. In small bowl whisk together juice, oil, mustard, lemon peel, vinegar, and pepper. Pour over vegetables and toss well.

Caprese Salad with Avocado

Serves 8–10

Ingredients

2 pints grape tomatoes, halved
3 tablespoons olive oil
1 clove garlic, chopped
¼ cup chopped fresh basil
2 (8 oz.) packages fresh mozzarella pearls
1 avocado, chopped
Sea salt and pepper (to taste)

Directions

In a large bowl, combine the tomatoes with the olive oil, garlic, and basil. Add mozzarella pearls and avocado and stir to coat.

Italian Chopped Salad

Serves 4

Ingredients

Vinaigrette
2 tablespoons olive oil
1 tablespoon red wine vinegar
Pinch salt and pepper

Salad
2 cups chopped spinach
3 cups chopped romaine
1 cup chickpeas, drained
¼ cup chopped salami
½ cup roasted, shredded chicken
½ cup shredded light mozzarella
½ cup chopped grape tomatoes

Directions

In a bowl whisk together olive oil and red wine vinegar. Add salt and pepper to taste.

In a large bowl mix the greens with chickpeas, salami, shredded chicken, cheese, and tomatoes. Add vinaigrette and toss to coat.

Italian Green Bean Salad

Serves 10

Ingredients

1 pound fresh green beans
1 (15 oz.) can red kidney beans, drained and rinsed
1 (15 oz.) can chickpeas, drained
1 medium-size purple onion
1 (6 oz.) can black olives, drained
¼ cup low-fat or fat-free Italian dressing of choice

Directions

Cut tips of green beans, and steam until crisp. Drain green beans and place in a serving bowl. Add the rest of the ingredients, and marinate overnight. Serve cold.

You may also add white kidney beans, yellow beans, or carrots.

Italian Salad with Roasted Grape Tomatoes and Italian Salad Dressing

Serves 6

Ingredients

Roasted Tomatoes
1 pint grape tomatoes
(about 1 cup)
2 tablespoons olive oil
Dash kosher salt
Dash smoked paprika

Salad
1 head of romaine lettuce, torn
1 small head radicchio, sliced thin
1 small red onion, sliced on mandolin
½ cup roasted red pepper slices (see Roasted Red Peppers on page 96)
2 ounces goat cheese
8 kalamata olives, sliced

Salad Dressing
(Makes about ½ cup)
⅓ cup olive oil
2 tablespoons white balsamic vinegar
Juice of ½ lemon
1 tablespoon each fresh parsley and oregano, finely chopped (if you need to use dried spices, use only 1 teaspoon each)
2 cloves garlic, minced
½ teaspoon Dijon mustard
Dash kosher or sea salt and ground pepper
Dollop honey (optional)

Directions

Toss all roasted tomato ingredients together and place on a parchment-lined cookie sheet. Bake at 325°F for about 30 minutes. Cool while preparing salad.

Put lettuce and radicchio together in a large bowl. Layer onions, peppers, and goat cheese on top of lettuce mixture. Add olives and roasted tomatoes. Toss with half of the dressing or leave on the side.

Put all salad dressing ingredients in a mason jar and shake until blended. Add honey if you would like a sweeter dressing. Refrigerate for 2 hours or longer. Take dressing out when you start to make the salad and tomatoes and bring to room temperature. Add 2 tablespoons to each serving.

Tri-Color Vegetable Pasta Salad

Serves 10

Ingredients

1 (16 oz.) box tricolor vegetable pasta, cooked according to instructions on box (do not overcook)

1 (5 oz.) can small black olives, sliced

1 cup raw broccoli, chopped into small pieces

1 cup finely chopped carrots

1 pint cherry tomatoes, halved (add to salad last)

½ cup fresh sliced mushrooms (optional)

½ low-fat or fat-free Italian salad dressing or balsamic vinaigrette dressing

Directions

Mix all ingredients together and chill.

White Bean Salad

Serves 6

Ingredients

2 cans cannellini beans, rinsed and drained
½ cup chopped red onion
¼ cup chopped fresh parsley
¼ cup olive oil
2 tablespoons red wine vinegar
2 tablespoons chopped fresh basil
Sea salt and pepper (to taste)

Directions

In large bowl mix cannellini beans with red onion and parsley. In a small bowl mix olive oil with red wine vinegar and fresh basil. Pour dressing over beans and marinate for at least an hour before serving.

Meat and Poultry Entrées

Chicken and Zucchini Marinara

Serves 4

Ingredients

4 tablespoons olive oil
½ small onion, chopped
2 cloves garlic, minced
¼ cup finely chopped carrot
2 cups crushed tomatoes
1 tablespoon each fresh parsley and basil
½ teaspoon salt
⅓ cup flour
4 chicken cutlets, pounded thin (put cutlets between wax paper, use a
meat-tenderizer tool, and pound until thin)
¼ cup white wine

Directions

Dip chicken breasts in egg and coat with breadcrumbs. Heat oil in a
covered 10-inch skillet. Add chicken. Brown on both sides over medium
heat. Combine marinara sauce with zucchini and pour over chicken.
Cover and simmer for 25 minutes or until chicken is tender. Sprinkle
with cheese before serving. Serve with favorite whole wheat pasta or
brown rice.

Chicken Cacciatore

Serves 4

Ingredients

4 tablespoons olive oil
½ small onion, chopped
2 cloves garlic, minced
¼ cup finely chopped carrot
2 cups crushed tomatoes
1 tablespoon each fresh parsley
and basil
½ teaspoon salt
⅓ cup flour

4 chicken cutlets, pounded thin
(put cutlets between wax paper,
use a meat-tenderizer tool, and
pound until thin)
¼ cup white wine

Directions

Sauté 2 tablespoons of olive oil with the onion, garlic, and carrots until
soft. Add crushed tomatoes, parsley, basil, and salt. Simmer for about
15 minutes. While sauce is simmering, floured cutlets, sauté in the
remaining 2 tablespoons of olive oil for about 7 minutes on each side
until cooked through. Add chicken and wine to sauce and cook on low
for another 20 minutes.

Chicken Cutlet Caprese

Serves 4

Ingredients

4 boneless chicken cutlets, pounded thin
¼ cup low-fat buttermilk
Italian-style panko breadcrumbs (you can substitute with whole wheat if you prefer)
3 tablespoons olive oil
2 cubes basil
1–2 tablespoons Locatelli Romano Cheese
2 Roma tomatoes, crushed (use food processor)
4 ounces fresh mozzarella, sliced

Directions

Preheat oven to 350°F. Dip the cutlets in buttermilk, and then in breadcrumbs. Heat 2 tablespoons of olive oil in a cast-iron pan. Cook cutlets until golden on both sides. Mix basil in a small bowl with the remaining tablespoon of olive oil. Add a sprinkle of the Romano cheese to the basil mixture. Leave aside. Pour the crushed tomatoes over the chicken cutlets. Put the mozzarella on top of each cutlet. Put in the oven and bake for about 15 minutes or until the cheese is melted. Swirl the basil mixture onto a serving platter. Put cutlets on the platter with juices from the pan. Sprinkle Romano cheese on the cutlets and serve.

Some grocery stores sell frozen basil in small cubes, or you can use 2 tablespoons of fresh basil that is finely chopped or 2 teaspoons of basil paste.

Chicken Italiano

Serves 4-6

Ingredients

2½–3 pounds boneless chicken, cut into small pieces
1 cup low-fat Italian dressing
Dash paprika
1 (4 oz.) can sliced mushrooms, drained, or ½ cup fresh mushrooms, sliced
⅓ cup Parmesan cheese
Sea salt and pepper (to taste)

Directions

Preheat oven to 350°F. Place chicken pieces in a large baking pan. Cover with ½ cup of dressing.

Sprinkle with paprika, salt, and pepper. Bake for 30 minutes. Turn chicken. Add mushrooms, ½ cup of dressing, cheese, and paprika. Bake 30 to 40 minutes, basting occasionally.

Chicken Oregano

Serves 4

Ingredients

1–3 pounds chicken, quartered
1 teaspoon salt
⅛ teaspoon black pepper
⅓ cup olive oil
4 tablespoons lemon juice
1 clove garlic, minced
1 teaspoon finely chopped parsley
2 teaspoons dried oregano

Directions

Place chicken skin-side up on a broiler pan. Sprinkle with salt and pepper. Combine the remaining ingredients and blend well. Broil under medium heat about 3 inches from the heat. Baste frequently for about 10 minutes. Turn chicken and sprinkle with salt and pepper. Baste again.

Continue to cook, basting frequently until the chicken is done. Check to make sure no pink juice appears when pricked with a fork.

Chicken Rosemary

Serves 6-8

Ingredients

2 cans small black olives
2 cans artichoke hearts in water (not marinade)
1 large, sliced onion
¼ cup olive oil
½ cup fresh rosemary, chopped
2 pounds chicken legs and thighs
3 cloves garlic, chopped
Sea salt and pepper (to taste)

Directions

In a large bowl, drain and empty the black olives. Drain and add the artichoke hearts. Add sliced onions, olive oil, salt, pepper, and half the rosemary. Let mixture set while cooking the chicken.

Coat a baking pan with olive oil and place chicken pieces in the pan. Sprinkle with salt, pepper, garlic, and the remainder of the rosemary. Cover and bake at 350°F for about an hour. Uncover and drain some liquid from the chicken (save if needed). Pour artichoke, olive, and onion mixture over chicken. Add some chicken liquid back into the pan and continue baking until chicken is done (about 15 to 20 minutes).

Chicken Saltimocca

Serves 4

Ingredients

4 boneless, skinless chicken cutlets
4 sage leaves
4 slices extra thin prosciutto
¼ cup flour
Olive oil spray
¼ cup white wine
¾ cup fat-free vegetable broth
1 tablespoon butter
Sea salt and pepper (to taste)

Directions

Pat chicken breasts with paper towels until dry. Pound chicken breasts until thin. Lay a sage leaf on top, and then a slice of prosciutto. Place flour in a bowl and lightly dredge the chicken, shaking off the excess. Heat a nonstick frying pan and spray with olive oil. Sauté chicken for 1 to 2 minutes on each side. Remove chicken from the pan and pour white wine in the pan to deglaze. Add vegetable broth and butter to the pan, and then add the chicken to the sauce. Finish cooking on low for 3 to 5 minutes until chicken is cooked through.

Zucchini Stuffed with Chicken-Apple Sausage, Peppers, and Onions

Serves 6

Ingredients

3 medium to large zucchinis, halved
4 links chicken sausage (such as Aidells® Chicken & Apple Sausage)
2 tablespoons olive oil
2 cloves garlic, minced
⅓ cup crushed tomatoes
1 teaspoon dried Italian seasoning

1 tablespoon grated Parmesan or Romano cheese
Olive oil cooking spray
2 ounces provolone slices, cut up
Sea salt and pepper (to taste)

Directions

Using a melon scooper, remove the insides from the zucchini, chop the inside meat, and leave zucchini boats aside (for stuffing). Remove casing from sausage and sauté in olive oil with minced garlic and chopped zucchini, breaking up the sausage as you cook it into crumbles. Cook on medium-low for about 12 to 15 minutes or until sausage is done. Add crushed tomatoes and seasoning and simmer on low for another 10 minutes for flavors to blend. Add Parmesan or Romano cheese and stir. Place zucchini boats in a glass baking dish, spray with olive oil cooking spray, and season with salt and pepper. Stuff each boat with sausage mixture. Top with chopped provolone. Bake at 350°F in a preheated oven for about 20 minutes or until zucchini boats are fork tender, but not mushy.

Turkey Sausage and Kale Lasagna

Serves 8

Ingredients

1 teaspoon salt
2 (10 oz.) bags kale, cut and cleaned
1 package sweet Italian turkey sausage
3 cups homemade pasta sauce (or store-bought)
3 tablespoons finely grated Parmesan cheese
1½ cups grated part-skim mozzarella cheese

Directions

Preheat oven to 375°F. Spray a 9- by 13-inch casserole dish with non-stick oil spray.

Bring a large pot of salted water to a boil. Add the kale to the boiling water, lower the heat, and cook the kale for 5 to 6 minutes. Drain kale in a colander. While the kale is cooking, heat a large nonstick frying pan, squeeze the sausage out of the casings, and sauté until the sausage is cooked through and browned. Add the pasta sauce, stir to combine, and let the sauce simmer for 20 minutes. In the lasagna dish, layer half the drained kale; sprinkle 1½ tablespoons of Parmesan cheese, half the sauce, and ¾ cup of mozzarella. Repeat until you have two layers of kale, Parmesan cheese, sauce, and mozzarella. Top with aluminum foil and bake for 30 minutes; then remove the foil and bake for another 15 minutes or until the cheese is bubbling. Let lasagna rest for 10 to 15 minutes before cutting and serving.

Cecilia's Turkey Meatballs

Serves 6

Ingredients

1 pound lean ground turkey
1 egg or equivalent egg beater
½ cup Italian seasoned breadcrumbs
½ cup instant oats (not flavored oats)
¼ cup chopped fresh parsley
Sea salt, pepper, and Mrs. Dash® Italian Medley Seasoning Blend
(to taste)

Directions

Mix all ingredients together in a large bowl. Roll and form medium-size meatballs. Place in favorite tomato sauce in a saucepan. Simmer for about 1 hour. Serve with favorite pasta.

Italian Sausage and Peppers

Serves 4

Ingredients

4 sweet or hot Italian turkey sausage links
1 green bell pepper, sliced
1 red bell pepper, sliced
1 sweet Vidalia onion, sliced
½ tablespoon olive oil
1 teaspoon Italian spices
4 whole wheat baguette rolls (optional)
Salt and pepper to taste

Directions

Heat a non-stick skillet on medium-high and cook the sausages until
brown on both sides (about 10 minutes). Remove and let drain on a
layer of paper towels. Heat olive oil in skillet over medium-heat; add
peppers and onions, season with Italian spices, salt and pepper and sauté
until onions are translucent. Toast baguette rolls in oven (optional).
Place sausage on a plate or roll, and top with peppers and onions to
serve.

Italian Meatloaf

Serves 6

Ingredients

1 pound extra lean ground beef
½ cup shredded zucchini
½ cup shredded carrots
½ cup white onion, diced
½ teaspoon dried Italian seasoning
½ teaspoon of garlic powder
1 cup of soft wheat breadcrumbs
1 can Italian style diced tomatoes (undrained)
2 egg whites, beaten
¼ cup of 2% mozzarella cheese, shredded
Olive oil spray

Directions

Heat oven to 375°F. Mix all ingredients except ¼ cup of mozzarella cheese until blended. Place mixture into a shallow loaf baking dish sprayed with cooking spray. Bake for1 hour or until done, topping with cheese during the last 10 minutes of cooking.

Polenta Parmesan

Serves 8

Ingredients

1 cup cornmeal
1 cup cold water
3½ cups boiling water
1 pound turkey sausage, removed from casing, crumbled, and browned in frying pan
2 cups marinara sauce
1 (8 oz.) package part-skim mozzarella cheese, shredded
½ cup grated Parmesan cheese
1 tablespoon fresh parsley, chopped
Sea salt and pepper (to taste)

Directions

Mix cornmeal and cold water together. Add mixture to boiling water and stir well. Let simmer for 8 minutes. After turkey sausage is cooked, drain and add to favorite tomato sauce. Simmer for 15 minutes. Spread cornmeal into a lightly greased baking dish. Grease with olive oil cooking spray. Chill for ½ hour. Sprinkle top of cornmeal with mozzarella cheese and chopped parsley, and then with sauce and sausage. Cover and heat for 35 minutes in a 350°F oven. Remove from the oven and let stand for 10 minutes. Sprinkle with grated cheese and cut into squares to serve.

Grilled Flank Steak with Tomatoes, Basil, and Arugula

Serves 6

Ingredients

Marinade
½ cup balsamic vinegar
¼ cup olive oil
2 cloves garlic, crushed
2 tablespoons honey
Sea salt and pepper (to taste)

Flank Steak
1½–2 pounds flank steak
Cooking oil spray
6 Roma tomatoes
2 tablespoons extra virgin olive oil
1 tablespoon fresh lemon juice
1 clove garlic, crushed
6 ounces baby arugula
Sea salt and pepper (to taste)

Directions

Marinate flank steak for 2 to 6 hours. Heat a gas grill, and then spray the grill with cooking oil spray. Drain steak and remove excess marinade. Grill steak 4 to 5 minutes until browned. Remove from grill and let rest for 5 minutes until you slice and serve.

Dice tomatoes and set aside. Mix 2 tablespoons olive oil with lemon juice, garlic, and a pinch of salt and pepper. Pour olive oil mixture over arugula and diced tomatoes. Top the arugula and tomatoes with warm slices of flank steak and serve.

Quadrettini Casserole

Serves 8

Ingredients

¼ cup margarine
¼ cup olive oil
½ cup finely chopped carrots
½ cup finely chopped onion
½ cup chopped celery
2 cloves garlic, chopped
1 pound lean ground beef or turkey
1 (16 oz.) can tomato paste
3 cups peeled and chopped tomatoes

2 teaspoons salt
1 teaspoon basil
½ teaspoon thyme
½ teaspoon Tabasco sauce
2 cups uncooked spinach noodles
1 (10 oz.) package frozen spinach
½ cup grated Parmesan cheese

Directions

Melt margarine in a large saucepan. Add oil, carrots, onions, celery, garlic, and meat (crumbled). Stir and cook until brown. Add tomato paste, tomatoes, salt, basil, thyme, and Tabasco sauce. Simmer uncovered for 1½ hours. Cook and drain noodles and spinach according to the respective packages. Add both to cooked mixture. Put in a 2-quart baking dish. Top with grated cheese. Cover with aluminum foil. Bake at 350°F for 20 minutes.

Note: This is a healthier version of the classic Chicken Parmesan. Turkey or pork cutlets can be substitutes.

Veal and Peppers

Serves 4

Ingredients

¼ cup olive oil
1–2 pounds veal cubes
3 medium-size peppers, cut up
2 cups favorite tomato sauce
Sea salt, pepper, parsley, and basil (to taste)

Directions

Pour olive oil in a Dutch oven. Add veal cubes to the pan and season. Brown veal cubes in olive oil for about 30 minutes on simmer. Add peppers and tomato sauce and simmer for another 30 minutes until veal is tender. Serve with brown rice.

Wine and Veal

Serves 4

Ingredients

10 thin veal cutlets
¼ cup flour
4 tablespoons olive oil
½ cup Marsala wine
¼ cup beef bouillon
Sea salt and pepper (to taste)

Directions

Stir wine into pan juices. Mix 1 tablespoon with bouillon. Add to the skillet. Cook over medium heat until thickened, stirring constantly. Pour over the cutlets. If desired, serve with stewed tomatoes.

Farro with Sausage and Apples

Serves 4

Ingredients

1 cup cooked farro, boiled in stock (vegetable or chicken)
3 sweet italian sausages, casings removed
1 tablespoon butter
1 cup diced onion
1 clove garlic, chopped
1 large apple, diced
Sea salt and pepper (to taste)
red chili flakes (to taste)

Directions

Set aside prepared farro. In a skillet add crumbled sausage and stir until browned, about 5 minutes. Remove sausage and save drippings. Add butter and melt. Add onion, garlic and apple, sauté until tender, about 5-6 minutes. Add sausage, salt, pepper and chili flakes. Stir until warmed, 1-2 minutes. Serve warm.

Seafood Entrées

Shrimp and Asparagus Bake

Serves 4

Ingredients

1 cup brown rice
2 tablespoons olive oil
1 pound fresh asparagus, cut into 1½-inch pieces
1 pound shrimp, peeled and deveined
2 cloves garlic, finely chopped
1 tablespoon lemon juice
Sea salt and pepper (to taste)

Directions

Cook rice according to the box and reserve. Heat olive oil and add asparagus. Stir for 3 minutes and remove asparagus from the skillet. Add shrimp and cook for 2 minutes. Stir in garlic, lemon juice, salt, and pepper. Stir in asparagus and rice. Heat through. Garnish with lemon wedges.

Shrimp Fra Diavolo

Serves 4

Ingredients

3 teaspoons extra virgin olive oil
6 cloves garlic, crushed
2 pounds jumbo shrimp, peeled and deveined
12 ounces whole wheat penne pasta
1 tablespoon onion powder
1 (35 oz.) can crushed tomatoes
1½ teaspoons crushed red pepper
1 tablespoon capers, drained
¼ cup fresh, chopped basil leaves
Sea salt and pepper (to taste)

Directions

Bring a large pot of salted water to a boil. While the water is heating up, heat 2 teaspoons of the olive oil in a large skillet over medium heat. Stir in the garlic and cook until golden brown. Add the shrimp and cook for 2 to 3 minutes (do not cook through); remove from the pan and sprinkle with salt to taste. Transfer the shrimp to a plate, leaving garlic in the pan.

Add pasta to water and cook according to the package directions for al dente. Add the remaining teaspoon of olive oil and add the onion powder and crushed tomatoes, season with salt and crushed red pepper, and bring to a simmer. Lower the heat and cook for about 10 minutes. Add the shrimp and cook for another minute or two; remove from heat. Add the capers and serve in a large bowl over pasta topped with fresh basil and Parmesan cheese.

Shrimp Scampi

Serves 2

Ingredients

1 tablespoon olive oil
6 cloves minced garlic
1 shallot, diced
1 pound large shrimp
¼ cup dry white wine
2 tablespoons lemon juice
2 tablespoons fresh Italian parsley, chopped

Directions

Heat a large skillet over medium heat and add olive oil. Add garlic, shallot, and shrimp, and cook until the shrimp starts turning pink. Add white wine and lemon juice and cook until most of the liquid has evaporated. Remove from heat and sprinkle with parsley.

Baked Clams

Serves 4

Ingredients

2 dozen littleneck clams
1 lemon
1 cup Italian breadcrumbs (or you can use the Homemade Breadcrumbs recipe on page 114 and add Italian seasoning)
2 tablespoons grated Parmesan or Romano cheese
1 teaspoon garlic powder
¼ cup light or whipped butter, melted
6 slices bacon (you can use low-sodium or turkey bacon if preferred)
1 tablespoon olive oil

Directions

Open clams and loosen from their shells. You can also put the clams on
a cookie sheet, bake at 375°F until they open, let cool, and then loosen
the clam meat from the shell. Squeeze the lemon over the clams. Melt
the butter and olive oil together and squeeze any remaining lemon
juice into the mixture. Mix the breadcrumbs with the cheese and garlic
powder. Fill each clam with the breadcrumb mixture; drizzle the butter
over the clams. Top with bacon and broil with an open oven door until
the bacon is cooked (7 to 10 minutes). Watch carefully so they do not
burn.

Grilled Scallops with Lemon Vinaigrette

Serves 4

Ingredients

Vinaigrette
¼ cup fresh lemon juice
1 tablespoon honey
1 tablespoon Dijon mustard
¼ cup olive oil
Sea salt and pepper (to taste)

Scallops
1¼ pounds sea scallops
2½ tablespoons olive oil
Cooking oil spray
Sea salt and pepper (to taste)

Directions

Combine the lemon juice, honey, mustard, salt, and pepper in a small bowl. Whisk ingredients while slowly pouring in the olive oil. Stir until thick. Heat a grill to medium-high. Spray the grill with cooking oil spray to prevent scallops from sticking. Toss the scallops with 2 tablespoons of olive oil in a small bowl. Put six scallops onto each skewer. Season with salt and pepper. Cook scallops for 2 to 3 minutes on each side.

Steamed Mussels in White Wine Broth with Sun-Dried Tomatoes and Fresh Basil

Serves 2

Ingredients

1½ pounds mussels
1 tablespoon olive oil
2 small shallots, sliced
Pinch salt and pepper
2 cloves garlic, minced
½ cup chopped sun-dried tomatoes (packed in water)
½ cup dry white wine
8 ounces chicken stock
2 tablespoons chopped basil

Directions

Clean and remove beards from mussels. Preheat a large pot to medium and add olive oil. Add sliced shallots and a pinch of salt and pepper; then cook for 5 minutes until the shallots have softened. Add garlic and tomatoes and cook for 1 minute. Add wine, chicken stock, and mussels; then cover with a lid and steam the mussels for 8 to 10 minutes or until all the mussels open (if any mussels do not open, discard). Garnish with fresh basil.

Fettuccine with Crabmeat

Serves 8

Ingredients

16 ounces whole wheat fettuccine
5 cloves garlic, chopped
Olive oil
½ cup chopped sun-dried tomatoes (in water)
½ pound lump crabmeat
½ cup crumbled ricotta salata
Pinch red pepper flakes
¼ cup chopped basil

Directions

Fill a large pot of water to a boil. Cook pasta according to the package directions till al dente. Sauté five chopped garlic cloves in olive oil for 2 to 3 minutes; then add the sun-dried tomatoes and crab and cook for another 2 minutes. Toss the cooked pasta with the garlic and olive oil mixture, ½ cup of ricotta salata, a pinch of red pepper flakes, and top with the chopped basil before serving.

Baked Flounder

Serves 2

Ingredients

Cooking spray
2 (4 oz.) flounder fillets
2 tablespoons fresh lemon juice
2 teaspoons canola oil
2 tablespoons dried whole wheat breadcrumbs
1 tablespoon Parmesan cheese
¼ cup Italian parsley, chopped
Sea salt and pepper (to taste)

Directions

Preheat oven to 350°F. Spray baking dish with nonstick cooking spray.
Place the fillets, skin-side down, in the baking dish. Add lemon juice
and canola oil on top of the fish. In a small bowl, combine the whole
wheat breadcrumbs, cheese, and pepper; sprinkle evenly over the fillets.
Bake for 15 minutes or until cooked through. Sprinkle with chopped
parsley and serve.

Filet of Sole Florentine

Serves 4

Ingredients

1 cup dry white wine
½ cup water
2 pounds fillet of sole
3 tablespoons extra virgin olive oil
2 tablespoons flour
½ teaspoon salt
1 (10 oz.) package frozen chopped spinach
¼ cup Pecorino Romano grated cheese

Directions

Combine wine and water in a large skillet and bring to a boil. Lower the heat and add the fillet of sole. Cook until the fish is flaky (about 10 minutes). Remove fish and keep warm. In small skillet add half the olive oil. Stir in flour and salt and blend. Gradually add wine mixture.

Cook over medium heat, stirring constantly until thickened. Spray an 8- by 11-inch baking dish with olive oil. Cook spinach according to the package, drain, and add to the baking dish. Arrange the fish fillets on the spinach. Pour the sauce over the fish. Sprinkle with grated cheese.

Bake in a hot oven at 450°F until the cheese is browned. Do not over-cook.

Tomato-Basil Salmon

Serves 4

Ingredients

4 (3 oz.) salmon fillets
½ cup grape tomatoes, halved
¼ cup extra virgin olive oil
½ cup fresh basil leaves, chopped
Sea salt and pepper (to taste)

Directions

Preheat oven to 400°F. Place aluminum foil or parchment paper on a baking pan.

Place salmon fillets skin-side down on the pan and season with salt and pepper. Mix tomatoes with olive oil, salt, and pepper. Top salmon fillets with tomato mixture and bake in a preheated oven for 15 minutes or until the salmon flakes easily with a fork. Let salmon rest for 3 to 5 minutes; top with fresh basil and serve.

Baked Tilapia and Tomatoes

Serves 4

Ingredients

2 teaspoons olive oil
2 pounds fresh tilapia
1 (6 oz.) can diced tomatoes (drain ½ juice)
2 teaspoons chopped fresh basil
2 teaspoons chopped fresh parsley
Mrs. Dash® Italian Medley Seasoning Blend (to taste)
Sea salt and pepper (to taste)

Directions

Coat a shallow baking pan with olive oil or spray with olive oil cooking spray. Lay tilapia fillets in the pan. Top with diced tomatoes, and sprinkle with basil, parsley, Mrs. Dash, salt, and pepper. Cook uncovered at 350°F for 10 to 15 minutes or until the fish is white and flaky. Serve with a green vegetable and brown rice.

Baked Tilapia Puttanesca

Serves 4

Ingredients

4 (5 oz.) tilapia fillets
Cooking spray
1 tablespoon extra virgin olive oil
2 cloves garlic, minced
⅓ cup chopped Italian parsley
¼ cup pitted, chopped kalamata olives
2 tablespoons capers
1 teaspoon anchovy paste
1 teaspoon dried oregano
⅛ teaspoon crushed red pepper flakes

Directions

Preheat oven to 350°F. Season tilapia with salt and pepper; coat a baking pan with cooking spray. Bake for 12 to 15 minutes until the tilapia flakes easily with a fork

Heat the oil in a large skillet over a medium heat. Add the garlic and sauté for 1 to 2 minutes. Add the parsley, olives, capers, anchovy paste, oregano, and crushed red pepper to the skillet, and sauté for 2 more minutes. Add the tomatoes and simmer for about 5 minutes. Pour the sauce over the tilapia fillets.

Baked Scallops in Breadcrumbs

Serves 3

Ingredients

1 teaspoon olive oil
12 large sea scallops
14 grape tomatoes
2 cloves of garlic
½ cup fresh whole wheat breadcrumbs
⅛ cup Parmesan cheese, grated
1 tablespoon Smart Balance butter
Juice of 1 lemon
Salt and pepper, to taste

Directions

Preheat the oven to 450°F. Pour a drizzle of olive oil into 2 gratin dishes and use your fingers to grease the inside of the dish. Place the scallops and tomatoes in an even layer between the two dishes, and season with salt and pepper.

Mix garlic, breadcrumbs, and Parmesan cheese in a food processor and process until well chopped. Add the butter and season with salt and pepper, and process until combined. Divide the breadcrumb mixture over the top of the scallops. Squeeze lemon over the top of the bread-crumbs on both gratin dishes. Place the dishes on a rimmed baking sheet, and bake until scallops are cooked through and breadcrumbs are golden brown (about 10 minutes).

Whole Wheat Spaghetti with Smoked Salmon

Serves 4

Ingredients

½ pound of whole wheat spaghetti
5 ounces smoked salmon
1 tablespoon olive oil
2 tablespoons lemon juice, fresh
1 teaspoon lemon zest
3 tablespoons capers
2 tablespoons Italian parsley, chopped
Salt and pepper, to taste
Grated parmesan for garnish

Directions

Cook pasta in a large saucepan according to packet instructions and drain. Return to pan; slice smoked salmon into thin strips. Stir olive oil and lemon juice through the pasta. Combine with lemon zest, capers, parsley and smoked salmon, stirring over low heat until warmed. Sprinkle with parmesan, salt and pepper.

Salmon Piccata

Serves 4

Ingredients

¼ cup flour
¼ teaspoon salt
¼ teaspoon black pepper
4 (3 oz.) salmon fillets
2 teaspoons butter
1 teaspoon olive oil
1½ cups white wine
2 tablespoons fresh lemon juice
2 tablespoons capers
¼ cup chopped fresh parsley

Directions

Preheat oven to 400°F. Combine flour, salt, and pepper; dredge salmon in flour mixture. Heat 1 teaspoon of butter and oil in a large skillet over medium-high heat.

Add salmon, browning both sides. Remove from the pan and bake covered in the oven for 10 to 15 minutes. Reserve liquid from the pan; add wine, 2 tablespoons of lemon juice, 1 teaspoon of butter, and capers to the pan, scraping up the brown bits and cooking for 2 minutes. Place salmon on serving plates, pour sauce over salmon, and top salmon fillets with chopped parsley

Spaghetti with Red Clam Sauce

Serves 4

Ingredients

8 ounces whole wheat spaghetti
¼ cup extra virgin olive oil
2 large cloves garlic, chopped
1 (15 oz.) can crushed tomatoes with basil
2 pounds littleneck clams
¾ cup dry white wine
Pinch crushed red pepper
Sea salt and pepper (to taste)
Parmesan cheese (to taste)

Directions

Bring a large pot of water to a boil. Cook pasta according to the package directions till al dente. Heat oil in a large saucepan over medium heat. Add garlic and cook, stirring for 2 to 3 minutes. Carefully add crushed tomatoes and bring to a simmer. Cook, stirring frequently until thickened slightly (about 5 minutes). In another pot bring clams and wine to a boil over high heat. Cover, reduce heat to medium, and cook until the clams open (4 to 6 minutes). Transfer the clams to a large bowl using a slotted spoon. Keep the clam broth and pour into the tomato sauce. Stir in crushed red pepper and simmer over medium heat for 1 minute. Season with salt and pepper. Pour the sauce over the pasta and top with clams. Serve with Parmesan cheese.

Pasta with Tuna, Lemon, and Capers

Serves 4

Ingredients

8 ounces whole wheat pasta shells
1 (6 oz.) can tuna (chunk or solid in olive oil), drained
1 large clove garlic, chopped
2 tablespoons fresh lemon juice
¼ cup olive oil
2 tablespoons capers, drained
Parmesan cheese
Sea salt and pepper (to taste)

Directions

Bring a large pot of water to a boil. Cook pasta according to the package directions till al dente. Stir together the tuna, garlic, lemon juice, olive oil, salt, pepper, and capers until combined. Drain pasta and add to tuna mixture while the pasta is hot. Serve with Parmesan cheese.

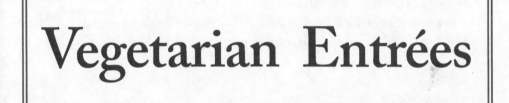

Vegetarian Entrées

Tofu Lasagna

Serves 8–10

Ingredients

1 (16 oz.) box whole wheat lasagna noodles
2 blocks soft tofu
⅔ egg, beaten with a fork
¼ cup grated Romano cheese
2 cups your favorite tomato sauce (either homemade or jarred)
Fresh parsley, basil, sea salt, and pepper (to taste)

Directions

Cook lasagna noodles according to the directions on the box. Mash tofu with a fork or potato masher until it is the consistency of Ricotta cheese. Blend tofu, eggs, cheese, and seasonings. Spread tomato sauce in the bottom of a lasagna pan. Layer lasagna noodle and tofu mixture, topping each layer with sauce and making sure the top layer is lasagna noodles, and cover with sauce. Sprinkle with additional Romano cheese and cover with foil. Bake at 350°F for 30 to 45 minutes; then let set for about 15 minutes before serving.

Easy Peas and Pasta

Serves 4–6

Ingredients

1 box small whole grain or wheat pasta shells
1 (12 oz.) package frozen baby peas
¼ cup light extra virgin olive oil
½ cup grated Romano cheese
Sea salt, pepper, and Mrs. Dash® Original Blend or Italian Medley
Seasoning Blend (to taste)

Directions

Cook pasta according to the directions on the box (do not overcook).
Cook peas according to the package (do not overcook). Mix together
with olive oil and seasonings, and top with grated cheese.

Garlic Pasta

Serves 4

Ingredients

8 cloves garlic
¼ cup olive oil
8 ounces spinach spaghetti, cooked according to directions
2 cups thinly sliced spinach
2 tablespoons whipped butter (or substitute with light butter)
Pecorino Romano cheese

Directions

Sauté garlic in olive oil until golden. Toss cooked pasta in the pan with the sautéed garlic. Toss in spinach and toss together. Add butter and toss until melted. Sprinkle with grated Romano cheese.

Artichoke and Tomato Cappellini

Serves 6

Ingredients

2 tablespoons chopped Vidalia onion
2 tablespoons minced fresh garlic
2 tablespoons extra virgin olive oil
1 (28 oz.) can Italian plum tomatoes, mashed
¾ cup low-salt chicken broth
3 tablespoons minced fresh parsley
1 (6 oz.) jar artichoke hearts, drained and chopped
1 cup whole wheat cappellini
Grated Romano cheese (to taste)
Sea salt and pepper (to taste)

Directions

In a large skillet cook onion and garlic in olive oil over low heat. Stir
until onion is soft. Add tomatoes with juice, chicken broth, parsley, salt,
pepper, and artichoke hearts and simmer for 10 to 15 minutes. In a large
saucepan cook cappellini until al dente and drain. Mix with sauce and
top with grated cheese and seasonings.

Fettuccine Alfredo

Serves 8

Ingredients

1 (16 oz.) package whole wheat fettuccine
1 small onion, diced
1½ tablespoons olive oil
1 (12 oz.) package soft tofu, drained
3 cloves garlic, minced
½ cup grated Parmesan cheese
Sea salt and pepper (to taste)

Directions

Cook pasta according to the package until al dente. In a small frying pan, sauté onion in ½ tablespoon of olive oil. In a food processor put tofu, garlic, cheese, sautéed onions, and 1 tablespoon of olive oil. Process until smooth. Place tofu mixture in a saucepan and warm. Mix pasta with tofu alfredo sauce.

Fettuccine Florentine

Serves 6-8

Ingredients

½ pound whole wheat fettuccine
1 package fresh spinach
¼ cup olive oil
¼ cup chopped parsley
⅛ cup basil
2 cloves chopped garlic
¼ grated Romano cheese
Sea salt and pepper (to taste)

Directions

Cook fettuccine according to the instructions on the box in a medium-size saucepan. Wash and steam spinach over low heat (add a little water to the saucepan). Drain fettuccine and return to the saucepan, adding spinach and the remaining ingredients. Toss together.

Note: You may double the recipe using 1 pound of fettuccini. You may also substitute spinach with broccoli or other favorite vegetable.

Mushroom Bolognese

Serves 8

Ingredients

2 teaspoons olive oil
1 clove garlic, crushed
2 large shallots, finely chopped
1 medium carrot, peeled and sliced
1 teaspoon dried oregano
2 cups presliced cremini mushrooms, chopped
1 (14 oz.) can crushed tomatoes
2 teaspoons Worcestershire sauce
¼ cup fat-free milk
1 (16 oz.) package whole wheat fettuccine

Directions

Heat oil in a large pan. Add garlic, shallots, and carrots; stir until onions are softened. Add oregano and chopped mushrooms and cook until soft. Pour in tomatoes and add Worcestershire sauce. Simmer for 25 minutes. Pour in milk, and simmer for another 10 minutes. Boil pasta according to the instructions on the package until *al dente*.

Green Spaghetti

Serves 4-6

Ingredients

3 cloves garlic
3 cups basil leaves
¼ cup extra virgin olive oil
Juice of ½ lemon
¼ cup low-sodium chicken broth
2 tablespoons pine nuts or walnuts
¼ cup Locatelli Romano cheese
1 (16 oz.) box whole grain or vegetable spaghetti (we like spinach)
4 ounces goat cheese or light cream cheese
Sea salt and pepper (to taste)

Directions

Pulse the garlic and basil leaves with the olive oil, lemon juice, and chicken broth until it is a paste. Add nuts and quickly pulse just to mince. Add half of the grated Romano cheese. Move to a large pasta bowl. Cook pasta according to the directions, but do not overcook. Save some of the spaghetti water. Put hot pasta in a bowl with the pesto and add goat cheese to the hot pasta. Stir until the cheese melts. Put the spaghetti water on the side and add a little if the mixture is too thick. Sprinkle with the remaining Romano cheese.

In our family we have a favorite dish called "green spaghetti." It is made of homemade pesto tossed with a block of cream cheese poured right onto the hot spaghetti. By accident we once substituted with goat cheese because we were out of cream cheese, and we loved the tangy taste the goat cheese added. It also saved a lot of fat calories. I added chicken broth to the pesto to reduce the fat as well.

Zucchini-Tomato Casserole

Serves 4

Ingredients

2 pounds tomatoes, sliced
1 pound zucchini, thinly sliced
2 cups mozzarella cheese, shredded
1 teaspoon salt
¼ teaspoon ground black pepper
2 tablespoons margarine

Directions

In a 2-quart casserole dish, layer tomatoes, zucchini, and cheese. Sprinkle each layer with salt and pepper. Finish casserole with tomatoes and cheese. Dot the top layer with margarine. Cover with foil and bake for 55 minutes at 350°F.

Tortellini Salad

Serves 4

Ingredients

½ pound three-blend vegetable tortellini with cheese
1½ cups chopped grape tomatoes
½ cup basil leaves
½ teaspoon fresh, finely chopped rosemary
¼ cup virgin olive oil
2 tablespoons white balsamic vinegar
2 tablespoons finely chopped red onion
⅓ cup roasted red peppers (see Roasted Red Peppers on page 96)
2 tablespoons shaved Locatelli Romano cheese

Directions

Cook tortellini according to the directions. Cool and toss with the remaining ingredients. Refrigerate or serve immediately at room temperature.

Eggplant Parmesan

Serves 6

Ingredients

1 large or 2 small eggplants
1 tablespoon kosher salt
Large bowl ice water
⅓ cup panko breadcrumbs
⅓ cup Italian breadcrumbs (your own or store-bought)
¼ cup Romano or Parmesan cheese
1 tablespoon Romano or Parmesan cheese

4 ounces fresh mozzarella, sliced
1 egg, combined with ⅓ cup water (egg wash)
Olive oil cooking spray
2 tablespoons olive oil
2 cups marinara sauce

Directions

Slice eggplants fairly thin. Add salt to water, place eggplant slices in cold salted water, and refrigerate for about 2 to 3 hours. Remove eggplant from water and drain between absorbent towels to remove as much moisture as possible. You can leave it for about an hour or longer between the towels.

Mix the breadcrumbs and cheese together and put on a plate. Put egg wash in a bowl. Put parchment paper on a cookie sheet and preheat oven to 350°F. Spray parchment paper with olive oil spray. Dip eggplant slices in egg wash, and then in breadcrumb mixture. Place on parchment paper. Drizzle half of the olive oil on the eggplant. Bake for about 10 minutes, turn slices, and drizzle with the remaining olive oil. Cook for about 10 more minutes until the eggplant is golden and soft. Remove the eggplant to a paper towel. Pour half of the marinara sauce in a baking pan (not metal). Layer eggplant slices; cover with the remaining sauce. Top with sauce; return to the oven for about 20 minutes. Remove from the oven and top with the remaining Romano or Parmesan cheese and mozzarella. Return to the oven and bake just until the cheese is melted (about 8 minutes).

You save fat and calories by baking the eggplant instead of frying it. You really don't lose much flavor, and the dish is much lighter. You can also eliminate the breadcrumbs for an even lighter dish. Just brush olive oil on the eggplant slices and bake on olive oil-sprayed parchment paper until soft.

Roasted Zucchinis and Tomatoes Parmigiano

Serves 4

Ingredients

4 tablespoons olive oil
2 cups grape tomatoes, crushed in food processor
4 cloves garlic, minced
Dash kosher salt
2–3 medium zucchinis, sliced thin
2 tablespoons finely chopped basil
2 ounces fresh mozzarella cheese (or use part-skim if desired)
1 tablespoon Parmesan cheese, grated

Directions

Prepare two cookie sheets covered with parchment paper; spray lightly with olive oil. Toss crushed tomatoes with 2 tablespoons of olive oil, garlic, and a dash of kosher salt. Put on one parchment-lined cookie sheet. Bake at 350°F for about 15 minutes before adding the zucchini sheet. Toss zucchini slices with the remaining olive oil and dash of kosher salt and place on the remaining parchment-lined cookie sheet. Put in the oven on a lower rack and bake both for 15 minutes while continuing to bake the tomatoes. Remove from the oven and place the zucchini in olive oil-sprayed glass cooking ware. Put the roasted tomato mixture over the zucchini. Add mozzarella and Parmesan cheese. Bake for about 8 to 10 minutes or just until the cheese has melted. Sprinkle with chopped basil and serve.

Spaghetti Squash Parmesan

Serves 4

Ingredients

2 medium-size spaghetti squash
1–2 cups favorite tomato sauce (homemade or prepared)
½ cup grated Parmesan or Romano cheese

Directions

Halve squash and scoop the seeds out. Place in a microwave on microwaveable plate facedown. Cook for about 10 minutes or until the skin is soft. Remove from the microwave and scoop out squash with a fork. Place on a plate and top with tomato sauce and cheese.

Note: You can substitute tomato sauce with ½ cup of olive oil and ½ cup of fresh basil.

Portobello Mushroom Pizzas

Serves 4

Ingredients

4 portobello mushrooms
1 cup spaghetti sauce
¼ cup Parmesan cheese
1 cup sliced black olives
1 cup part-skim mozzarella
8 small slices meatless pepperoni

Directions

Preheat the oven to 375°F. Put mushrooms on a baking sheet and bake for 5 minutes. Remove from the oven, spread spaghetti sauce evenly over the mushroom caps, top with Parmesan cheese, olives, mozzarella, and meatless pepperoni. Bake for an additional 20 minutes.

Farro with Red Pepper and Mushrooms

Serves 4

Ingredients

1 cup cooked farro, boiled in stock (vegetable)
3 tablespoons olive oil
red chili flakes (to taste)
1 red bell pepper, diced
1 cup mushrooms, diced
1 cup diced onion
1 clove garlic, chopped
½ cup vegetable or mushroom broth
1 tablespoon butter
Sea salt and pepper (to taste)

Directions

Set aside prepared farro. In a skillet add olive oil and red pepper flakes, sauté for 2 minutes. Add red pepper, mushrooms and onion and sauté until lightly browned. Add broth slowly and stir for 1-2 minutes. Add farro, butter and stir until sauce is slightly thickend, about 2 minutes. Season with salt and pepper. Serve warm.

Side Dishes

Roasted Red Peppers

Serves 6

Ingredients

4 large red peppers
Olive oil cooking spray
1 tablespoon olive oil
1 teaspoon unfiltered vinegar or vinegar of your choice (balsamic vinegar will sweeten the peppers a bit)
2 cloves garlic, finely chopped
1 teaspoon Italian seasoning

Directions

Preheat oven to 450°F. Cut red peppers into quarters. Place on parchment paper sprayed with olive oil cooking spray. Bake for about 15 minutes; then broil until skins start to blacken. Remove from oven and, using tongs, place in a brown paper bag, roll the bag closed, and let the peppers cool a bit. Remove skins and slice into strips. Put in a container and add oil, vinegar, garlic, and seasoning. Store in a refrigerator or freezer for later use.

Note: These are great in salads or on pizza or pasta. If the peppers are bought during the summer months, they can be frozen in bags for use all year.

Stuffed Peppers

Serves 4-6

Ingredients

6 green or red medium-size peppers
1 pound lean ground turkey
1 egg or egg beater equivalent
1 cup brown rice
½ cup instant oats
1 (29 oz.) can tomato puree
1 (29 oz.) can crushed tomatoes
Sea salt, pepper, garlic powder, and Mrs. Dash® Original Blend (to taste)
Parmesan or Romano cheese (to taste)

Directions

Cut top of each pepper, removing stems and seeds, and rinse inside of pepper with cool water. Mix turkey, egg, rice, oats, and seasonings in a large bowl. Stuff each pepper with mixture to top of opening. Add about 1 to 2 inches of water in a large pot or Dutch oven. Place stuffed peppers in pot and cover; then let simmer for 20 to 30 minutes. Add tomato purée and crushed tomatoes over peppers. Season to taste. Simmer peppers until tender and meat is cooked (about ½ hour). Garnish with grated cheese when serving.

Stuffed Tomatoes

Serves 6

Ingredients

6 medium tomatoes
2 tablespoons olive oil
1 tablespoon whipped butter
3 cloves garlic, chopped
½ small red onion, chopped
½ cup breadcrumbs
½ cup panko breadcrumbs
2 tablespoons Romano cheese
2 tablespoons fresh basil, chopped fine
1 tablespoon fresh parsley, chopped fine
2 ounces provolone cheese, cut into 6 pieces

Directions

Cut tops off tomatoes and scoop out the meat, leaving the shell. Finely chop the tomato pulp. Heat 1 tablespoon of olive oil and 1 tablespoon of whipped butter in a frying pan. Sauté the garlic and onion on low until soft. Add tomato pulp and heat on low for about 5 minutes. Mix breadcrumbs and cheese. Add to the pan and stir until blended. Remove from heat and cool slightly. Add the herbs and stir. Fill up the tomato cups with the mixture, place a piece of provolone on top of each tomato, and drizzle with the remaining tablespoon of olive oil. Bake at 350°F for about 20 minutes or until the tomatoes are soft, but not mushy.

Green Tomato Pizza Bites

Serves 4-6

Ingredients

2 tablespoons olive oil
2 cloves garlic, minced
1 teaspoon Italian seasoning
2 green tomatoes, sliced in medium slice rings
Olive oil spray
2 tablespoons grated Romano or Parmesan cheese
4 ounces fresh mozzarella cheese

Directions

Mix the olive oil, garlic, and seasoning together and let it sit to blend. Place tomato slices on oil-sprayed parchment paper on a cookie sheet. Drizzle the garlic oil over the tomatoes and top with Romano cheese and mozzarella pieces. Bake at 350°F until the cheese melts and tomatoes are fork tender.

Shredded Zucchini

Serves 4

Ingredients

5–6 medium zucchini squash (or combine yellow and zucchini squash)
3 cloves garlic, sliced thin
3 tablespoons olive oil
Freshly shaved Romano cheese
Sea salt and pepper (to taste).

Directions

Shred the zucchini and place between towels to dry out a bit. Get as much moisture out as possible. Sauté thinly sliced garlic in olive oil until soft. Add the dried shredded squash and stir well to blend the oil and garlic mixture into the squash. Turn on low and continue to stir often.

Cook for about 10 minutes or until the squash wilts slightly. Remove from heat and put into a serving bowl. Top with shaved cheese.

Zucchini Ribbons with Garlic and Goat Cheese

Serves 4

Ingredients

1 tablespoon olive oil
2 large zucchinis, shaved with potato peeler
2 ounces goat cheese
1 tablespoon fresh lemon juice
Sea salt and pepper (to taste)

Directions

Heat olive oil in a pan; add zucchini ribbons, sauté for 3 minutes, and add goat cheese until melted. Squeeze fresh lemon juice on top; add salt and pepper to taste.

Roasted Garlic and Cauliflower

Serves 6

Ingredients

4 tablespoons extra virgin olive oil
1 large cauliflower
⅛ teaspoon dried basil
4 cloves garlic, crushed
¼ cup Pecorino Romano cheese

Directions

Coat the bottom of the baking sheet with half of the olive oil. Break cauliflower into flowerets. Place in a bowl and mix with the remaining olive oil, basil, and garlic. Place cauliflower flowerets on the baking sheet. Bake at 400°F for 10 minutes. Sprinkle with cheese before serving.

Ricotta-Topped Garlic Bread

Serves 4

Ingredients

4 cloves garlic
4 tablespoons olive oil
1 small loaf whole wheat baguette bread, sliced about 1¼ inches thick
1 cup low-fat or fat-free ricotta cheese
1 tablespoon Parmesan or Romano cheese (remove from refrigerator and let sit for about 20 minutes at room temperature)
2 teaspoons fresh chopped parsley
1 tablespoon white balsamic vinegar

Directions

Blend the garlic cloves and olive oil in a food processor. Preheat oven to 350°F. Brush the bread with the garlic oil and place on parchment paper. Bake for about 10 minutes or until toasted. Mix the ricotta cheese with the Parmesan or Romano cheese and parsley. Put a small mound on the warm garlic bread, drizzle balsamic vinegar, and serve immediately.

Note: Also makes a tasty, quick little appetizer or lunch.

Lemon Juice and Broccoli

Serves 6

Ingredients

2 pounds broccoli or 2 (10 oz.) packages frozen broccoli
2 tablespoons olive oil
⅓ cup celery, chopped
¼ cup pimentos, chopped
2 tablespoons lemon juice
¼ teaspoon salt
⅛ teaspoon pepper

Directions

Wash and trim broccoli. Cook in water for 15 minutes or cook frozen broccoli according to the package directions. Heat olive oil in a skillet. Sauté celery for 1 minute. Stir in the remaining ingredients. Drain the broccoli, and pour the mixture over the broccoli.

Whole Wheat Pasta with Broccoli

Serves 4

Ingredients

1 (32 oz.) carton chicken broth
1 (8 oz.) package whole wheat penne pasta
3 cups raw broccoli
Red pepper, crushed
¼ cup Parmesan cheese

Directions

In large pot boil chicken broth and cook pasta in chicken broth until al dente. With slotted spoon remove pasta. Add broccoli to chicken broth until soft. Spoon broccoli and chicken broth over pasta; top with crushed red pepper and Parmesan cheese.

Broccoli Rabe

Serves 4

Ingredients

1 large bunch broccoli rabe
3 cloves garlic, minced
3 tablespoons olive oil
Juice of ½ lemon
Shaved Romano cheese
½ teaspoon hot red pepper flakes (optional)
Sea salt (optional)

Directions

Cook broccoli rabe in boiling water for about 2 minutes. Remove and place in a colander and rinse with cold water. Place on a towel to dry. Sauté garlic in olive oil until soft. Add broccoli rabe and sauté until warmed through. Squeeze lemon over the rabe and put in a serving dish. Put shaved cheese on top and sprinkle with red pepper flakes. Salt if needed (the cheese adds salt so no more than a small amount should be added).

Roasted Radishes

Serves 4

Ingredients

15–20 small to medium red radishes
2 tablespoons olive oil
1 teaspoon finely chopped rosemary
Dash thyme
2 cloves minced garlic
Sea salt and pepper (to taste)

Directions

Mix all ingredients in a bowl. Place on parchment paper on a cookie sheet. Bake at 375°F for about 20 minutes or until the radishes are fork tender. Turn several times during baking.

Roasted Vegetables

Serves 6

Ingredients

½ cup olive oil
1 head cauliflower
1 bunch broccoli
1 bunch asparagus
3 cloves garlic, chopped
Sea salt and pepper (to taste)

Directions

Coat a baking pan with oil. Toss vegetables with oil and place vegetables on the pan. Add garlic cloves.

Stuffed Artichokes

Serves 4

Ingredients

4 artichokes
⅓ cup homemade whole wheat breadcrumbs
2 tablespoons grated Parmesan or Romano cheese
½ teaspoon garlic powder
Juice of 1 lemon
2 tablespoons olive oil

Directions

Cut artichoke leaves to remove their pointy parts. Cut off stems. On hard surface, leaf-side down, firmly press until artichoke opens. Mix the breadcrumbs, cheese, and garlic powder together. Squeeze the lemon among the four artichokes, trying to get between the leaves. Fill the center and the spaces in between the leaves with the breadcrumb mixture. Put into a saucepan that will accommodate the four artichokes so they are touching and standing upright. Drizzle the artichokes with the olive oil and bring to a boil. Lower heat to medium-low, cover, and cook for about 2 hours or until the leaves are tender. Be careful to watch that the water level does not get too low. Add water as needed. (These can also be made in a Crock-Pot®, cooking all day on low.)

Stuffed Mushrooms

Serves 2

Ingredients

1 cup finely chopped tomatoes
2–3 cloves garlic
2 tablespoons olive oil
1 teaspoon chopped fresh basil
2 ounces fresh mozzarella, chopped into cubes
1 portobello mushrooms
1 tablespoon shaved Romano cheese
Dash kosher salt (optional)

Directions

Mix the tomatoes, garlic, and 1 tablespoon of olive oil together. Toss in basil and mozzarella, as well as a dash of kosher salt if desired. Drizzle the remaining tablespoon of oil on the mushrooms. Fill with the tomato-to-cheese mixture. Spray parchment paper with olive oil cooking spray and place stuffed mushrooms on the paper. Bake at 350°F for about 20 minutes. Sprinkle with shaved Romano cheese and serve. You can also return the stuffed mushrooms to the oven for about 10 minutes if you prefer the tomato mixture to be warm.

Black Olives and Celery

Serves 4

Ingredients

2 (6 oz.) cans small black pitted olives
6 stalks green celery, chopped finely
2–4 tablespoons extra virgin olive oil
3 cloves garlic, chopped finely, or 1 tablespoon minced garlic from a jar
Sea salt and pepper (to taste)

Directions

Mix all ingredients together. Serve with favorite Italian meal as a side dish.

Carrots and Anise

Serves 6

Ingredients

1 pound carrots
2 tablespoons margarine
½ teaspoon crushed anise seed
¼ cup orange juice

Directions

Peel carrots. Cut diagonally into half-slices. Cook carrots in 1 inch of boiling water for about 10 to 12 minutes or until tender. Drain and return to pot. Add margarine and anise seed. Cook for 1 minute. Stir in orange juice. Cook for 1 to 2 minutes or until heated through.

Goat Cheese Bruschetta

Serves 8

Ingredients

2 tablespoons olive oil
½ teaspoon garlic granules or powder
Dash smoked paprika
Dash kosher salt
8 slices multigrain baguette bread (or any loaf of bread of your choice)
8 ounces goat cheese, sliced into rounds
½ cup roasted red peppers (see Roasted Red Peppers on page 96), thinly sliced
¼ cup honey

Directions

Preheat oven to 350°F. Mix olive oil and seasonings together. Place bread slices on parchment paper and brush oil mixture on bread slices. Bake at 350°F for about 10 minutes or until lightly toasted. Remove from oven and place 1 round of goat cheese on each bread piece. Layer the red pepper slices on top. Drizzle with honey and return to the oven for about 5 minutes (just enough to warm the cheese). Serve immediately.

Homemade Breadcrumbs

Serves 6

Ingredients

8 ounces bread (healthier choice would be whole grain or whole wheat)
1½ tablespoons dried Italian seasoning

Directions

Tear up and toast the bread in a 350°F oven until golden (about 15 minutes). Cool toast and put in a food processor. Add the Italian seasoning and pulse until made of fine crumbs. (You can add garlic powder or onion powder if you like.) You can freeze the crumbs in freezer bags if desired.

Italian Corn

Serves 6

Ingredients

2 tablespoons olive oil
½ teaspoon oregano
6 ears husked corn
Sea salt and pepper (to taste)

Directions

Preheat oven to 350°F. Mix olive oil with salt, pepper, and oregano. Roll corn cobs in mixture. Place on parchment paper and bake for about 20 minutes, turning often.

Note: Everyone will love this baked corn—and there's no need for butter!

Artichoke Pie

Serves 6

Ingredients

6 tablespoons egg beaters
1 egg
½ cup ricotta cheese
4 ounces mozzarella cheese
8 ounces chopped artichoke hearts, frozen, and cooked according to directions on bag
1 teaspoon Italian seasoning
2 tablespoons grated Romano or Parmesan cheese
1 cup of finely chopped arugula
Olive oil cooking spray
Sea salt and pepper (to taste)

Directions

Mix all ingredients together and spray a glass pie plate with olive oil cooking spray. Pour into the pie plate and cook at 350°F for about 30 minutes or until set. Let it sit until slightly cooled before slicing.

Peaches in Wine

Serves 8

Ingredients

4 large peaches
1 teaspoon Splenda®/stevia
8 ounces prosecco

Directions

Peel and slice peaches into thin slices. Add Splenda/stevia to peaches and mix together. Pour prosecco over peaches to serve.

Sauces and Dressings

Tasty Tomato Sauce

Serves 8

Ingredients

1 (28 oz.) can San Marzano organic peeled tomatoes
1 (28 oz.) can crushed tomatoes with basil
1 (28 oz.) can tomato puree
2 peeled carrots, cut into thirds
2 cloves garlic, chopped
1 bay leaf
¼ cup fresh parsley, finely chopped
Mrs. Dash® Italian Medley Seasoning Blend (to taste)
Sea salt and pepper (to taste)

Directions

Mash the peeled tomatoes using a potato masher. In a large pot, add all ingredients together. Simmer for 1½ hours, stirring occasionally. Serve over favorite pasta.

Note: You can also add the carrots to the sauce to cut the acid instead of adding sugar.

Fresh Marinara Sauce

Makes 3 cups

Ingredients

12–15 plum tomatoes, skins removed and seeded
2 tablespoons olive oil
4 cloves garlic, minced
¼ teaspoons of oregano, parsley, and basil (when in season, you can use fresh herbs, finely chopped, but add them after sauce simmers awhile and is ready to serve)
¼ cup dry red wine (optional)
⅓ cup finely chopped onion (optional; if using onion, cook in olive oil until lightly browned, and then add garlic)
Sea salt and pepper (to taste)

Directions

Boil water in a saucepan and put tomatoes in boiling water for about 20 seconds. Remove and put into a bowl of ice water. Remove after about 30 seconds and put into another bowl. Remove skins, open the tomatoes, and press out as many seeds as possible over a strainer in another bowl to reserve the juice.

Sauté garlic in olive oil on medium-low heat until soft, but not brown. Pour reserved tomato juice into the saucepan with garlic. Put tomatoes in a food processor and pulsate until crushed. Pour into the saucepan. Add herbs, salt, and pepper to taste. Simmer for about 2 hours on very low or in a Crock-Pot on low until sauce thickens.

Variation: Marinara Sauce from canned crushed tomatoes with paste. You can also substitute 1 (28 oz.) can of good-quality crushed tomatoes (Pomi, Muir Glen, Cento, or Trader Joe's plum tomatoes) and 1 can of tomato paste instead of fresh tomatoes.

Buttermilk-Pesto Vinaigrette

Makes 1 cup

Ingredients

1 cup basil
¼ cup parsley
2–3 cloves garlic
¼ cup olive oil
⅓ cup low-fat buttermilk
2 tablespoons light mayonnaise
1 tablespoon apple cider vinegar
Juice of ½ lemon
1 tablespoon Dijon mustard
¼ teaspoon kosher salt
⅓ teaspoon ground black pepper

Directions

Blend basil, parsley, garlic, and oil in a food processor until smooth. Whisk the remaining ingredients together and pour into the pesto. Stir to blend. Refrigerate for at least 2 hours to blend flavors.

Can be used in a pasta salad or as a salad dressing. Use 2 tablespoons per serving.

Simple Pasta Pesto

Serves 6

Ingredients

2 cups fresh basil leaves
2–4 cloves garlic, chopped
¼ cup pine nuts
¼ cup grated Romano cheese

Directions

Blend all ingredients in a blender or food processor (Magic Bullet™ is a good one to use). Pour mixture over favorite whole wheat or multigrain pasta, and sprinkle with Romano cheese.

White Clam Sauce

Makes 4 cups
Serves 6

Ingredients

3 cloves minced garlic
¼ cup sun-dried tomatoes, finely chopped (in bag, not oil; follow directions to rehydrate)
1 small Vidalia onion, finely chopped
2 bottles clam juice
2 cans minced clams
1 cup good-quality chicken broth or your own homemade broth
½ cup dry white wine

12 ounces whole wheat or whole grain linguine
1 dozen littleneck clams, scrubbed
2 tablespoons fresh parsley
Juice of 1 lemon
2 tablespoons olive oil
¼ cup grated Parmesan or Romano cheese
Red pepper flakes

Directions

Sauté garlic, rehydrated tomatoes, and onions in olive oil until soft. Add clam juice, minced clams, chicken broth, and juice of one lemon, and simmer for about 10 minutes for flavors to mingle. Add wine. Cook linguine. Add littleneck clams and simmer on low until they open. Pour sauce over linguine, add fresh parsley, and put clams on top. Serve with grated Romano or Parmesan cheese and red pepper flakes.

Blue Crab Sauce

Makes 4 cups
Serves 6

Ingredients

3 cloves garlic, crushed
3 tablespoons olive oil
1½ dozen small blue crabs, cleaned
1 teaspoon red pepper flakes
2 large cans crushed tomatoes
1 teaspoon oregano
¼ cup dry red wine
1 pound spinach linguine
Grated cheese for pasta

Directions

Sauté the garlic in olive oil until soft. Add crabs and sauté, turning until warmed. Add the remaining ingredients, cover the pot, stirring frequently, and cook on low for about 20 minutes. Serve over spinach linguine.

Low-Calorie Shrimp Marinara

Serves 4

Ingredients

5 cloves garlic, sliced
¼ cup olive oil
1 (16 oz.) can tomato puree
½ cup chopped fresh parsley
¼ cup fresh chopped basil
1 pound shrimp, shelled and cleaned
½ pound whole grain or whole wheat pasta
¼ cup grated Parmesan cheese
Sea salt and pepper (to taste)

Directions

In large skillet heat garlic and olive oil over low heat for about 6 minutes or until the garlic is soft. Add tomato puree, parsley, basil, salt, and pepper, and let simmer for 10 minutes. Add shrimp and cook until pink over medium heat. Serve over cooked pasta and sprinkle with grated cheese.

Note: Recommended pasta choices are cappellini, linguini, rotini, tricolor rotini, and large shells. Ronzoni Smart Taste pasta has increased fiber, calcium, and vitamin D.

Balsamic Vinaigrette

Serves 6

Ingredients

¾ cup extra virgin olive oil
¼ cup balsamic vinegar
Sea salt and pepper (to taste)

Directions

Mix all ingredients together; serve over fresh greens or as a dipping sauce for bread.

Creamy Italian Dressing

Serves 8

Ingredients

¾ cup Greek yogurt
¼ cup sour cream
2 tablespoons milk
¼ teaspoon dry mustard
¼ teaspoon Italian herb blend
Pinch garlic powder
Sea salt and black pepper (to taste)

Directions

Mix all ingredients together and chill for at least 1 hour before serving.
Makes 1 cup.

Marsala Sauce

Serves 4

Ingredients

2 tablespoons olive oil
1 large shallot, chopped
2 cloves garlic, diced
1 (10 oz.) package white mushrooms, sliced
¼ cup flour
1½ cups chicken broth
¾ cup Marsala wine
¼ cup Italian parsley, chopped

Directions

Heat olive oil in a saucepan; add shallot and garlic until fragrant (2 to 3 minutes). Add mushrooms; cook for 3 to 4 more minutes. Mix flour with chicken broth in a separate bowl. Slowly add the flour-chicken broth mixture, stirring consistently till the sauce thickens. Add Marsala wine, cook on a simmer for 5 minutes, and add parsley right before serving.

Desserts

Prosecco and Peaches

Serves 4

Ingredients

6 fresh, ripe peaches
1 teaspoon honey or brown sugar
1 teaspoon cinnamon
½ bottle good-quality prosecco
Fat-free whipped cream
Mint leaves (for garnish)

Directions

Peel and slice the peaches rather thin. Toss with honey and cinnamon.
Place in wine glasses. Pour prosecco over the fruit and top with a dollop
of whipped cream and fresh mint leaves. Serves six small or four large
wineglasses.

Baked Apples

Serves 6

Ingredients

6 Granny Smith apples
2 tablespoons light or whipped butter
1 tablespoon brown sugar or sugar substitute equivalent to 2 table-spoons
1 tablespoon honey
1 teaspoon ground cinnamon
⅓ cup chopped walnuts
⅓ cup raisins
⅓ teaspoon lemon juice
¼ cup fresh apple cider

Directions

Spray a glass baking pan with cooking spray. Slice apples into wedges; remove skin. Toss all ingredients together. Cover with foil and bake at 350°F for about 25 minutes or until apples are fork tender. Serve with low-fat ice cream or frozen yogurt.

Strawberries in Balsamic Vinegar

Serves 4

Ingredients

2 cup chopped strawberries
3 tablespoons balsamic vinegar
1 tablespoon stevia/Splenda®

Directions

Chop strawberries into two or four pieces (depending on their size), and then place them in a bowl. Add the balsamic vinegar and stevia/Splenda to the strawberries; then cover the bowl and shake it gently so the fruit is evenly coated with the vinegar. Let strawberries marinate for at least 15 minutes before serving.

Minted Strawberries

Serves 6

Ingredients

15–20 strawberries, hulled and sliced
½ cup chocolate mint leaves
(if you cannot find them, then use regular mint leaves)
1 tablespoon sugar
2 tablespoons limoncello or liqueur of your choice
(Kahlúa® is good too)

Directions

Mix together and let marinate a while. You can use as a topping on light ice cream, frozen yogurt, or angel food cake for a light dessert.

Espresso Pudding

Serves 8

Ingredients

4 cups skim milk
3.9 ounces instant sugar-free chocolate pudding mix
3.9 ounces instant sugar-free vanilla pudding mix
1½ cups instant espresso, cooled

Directions

Follow instructions on pudding mix packages to prepare pudding using skim milk. Follow instructions to prepare instant espresso. Pour the espresso into the vanilla pudding. In plastic drink cups, layer espresso/vanilla pudding with the chocolate pudding. Chill until it sets, and then serve.

Coffee and Cream

Serves 1

Ingredients

1 scoop good-quality low-fat ice cream or frozen yogurt
Espresso or other strong coffee (World Market® Italian Blend is a
good one)
Dark chocolate chips (to taste)
Fat-free whipped cream (to taste)

Directions

Put one scoop of ice cream in a coffee cup. Pour coffee into the cup.
Sprinkle a few chocolate chips on top and squirt a dash of whip cream.
Really hits the spot when you want something rich without a lot of fat
and calories.

Zucchini Bread

Serves 12

Ingredients

3 cups white whole wheat flour

2 teaspoons cinnamon

½ teaspoon nutmeg

1 teaspoon baking soda

1 teaspoon baking powder

¾ teaspoon kosher salt

2 eggs

3 tablespoons egg beaters

¼ cup honey

⅓ cup olive oil, or canola oil, or coconut oil

¾ cup light brown sugar

3 teaspoons real vanilla extract

1 cup smooth applesauce

¾ cups chopped walnuts

½ cup raisins

2½ cups shredded zucchini

Directions

Preheat oven to 325°F. Spray two loaf pans, and then flour the pans. Mix dry ingredients together. Beat the eggs, egg beaters, honey, oil, sugar, vanilla, and applesauce. Add dry mixture and nuts, raisins, and zucchini. Bake for about 45 to 50 minutes. Check by inserting a long toothpick or something similar into the center of the bread until it comes out clean. Let cool before slicing.

Mock Cannoli Pudding

Serves 4 large or 6 small

Ingredients

8 ounces part-skim or fat-free ricotta cheese
½ teaspoon orange peel, grated
1 tablespoon orange juice
1 tablespoon honey
1 ounce Frangelico® liqueur or liqueur of your choice
¼ cup mini semisweet chocolate chips
2 tablespoons slivered almonds or chopped pistachio nuts
Dash dark cocoa powder

Directions

Blend together all the ingredients *except* the chocolate chips, almonds, and cocoa powder. Put mixture in small cups or wineglasses. Sprinkle the cocoa powder on top, and then the chocolate chips and almonds.

Ricotta Cheesecake Parfaits

Serves 4

Ingredients

2 cups part-skim ricotta cheese
2 teaspoons vanilla extract
1 teaspoon Splenda®
1 tablespoon honey
1 cup reduced-fat graham crackers, crumbled

Directions

In a bowl, mix together ricotta cheese, vanilla extract, Splenda, and honey until combined. Set aside in a fridge. In a bowl, layer graham cracker crumbs and ricotta mixture. Top with your favorite fresh berries.

Basil-Lemon Shaved Ice

Serves 8

Ingredients

1 cup white sugar
Water
30 basil leaves

Directions

Dissolve 1 cup of white sugar in 1 cup of water in a small saucepan. Add about 30 basil leaves to the saucepan; bring to a boil. Once the water boils, turn to a low simmer for 10 minutes, stirring frequently. On low heat, cover and let sit for 20 more minutes. Using a strainer, pour the liquid into a jar. Fill a small bowl with crushed or shaved ice, and spoon a couple of tablespoons of the basil simple syrup over the top.

Citrus Italian Ice

Serves 6–8

Ingredients

2 cups water
½ cup honey
¼ cup lemon juice (1 lemon)
¼ cup orange juice (½ an orange)
½ teaspoon grated lemon peel
½ teaspoon grated orange peel

Directions

Mix all ingredients and bring to a boil. Cool and pour into 4-ounce plastic cups. Freeze; then remove from the freezer and keep at room temperature until it starts to become slushy. Serve.

Gelato

Serves 4

Ingredients

¼ cup stevia, Splenda®, or honey
32 ounces nonfat Greek yogurt

Directions

Whisk the stevia, Splenda, or honey into the yogurt. Freeze with an ice-cream maker.

Macaroons

Makes 18 small cookies

Ingredients

1 cup blanched almonds, put through food processor
⅓ cup sugar
2 egg whites
½ teaspoon almond extract
Dash kosher salt

Directions

Process almonds and add sugar in a food processor (should look like paste). Beat egg whites until stiff peaks form. Mix the almond powder with the sugar. Fold in the egg whites and almond extract. Place parchment paper on a cookie sheet and lightly spray with cooking spray. Place rounded teaspoons onto the sprayed parchment paper. Preheat oven to 300°F and bake until lightly brown (about 20 minutes).

Resources

Eating Well
www.eatingwell.com

Italian Food Forever
www.italianfoodforever.com

LIVESTRONG
www.livestrong.com

Made-in-Italy.com
www.made-in-italy.com

SimpleItalianCooking.com
www.simpleitaliancooking.com

The World's Healthiest Foods
www.whfoods.com

My Recipes

My Recipes

My Recipes

My Recipes

My Recipes

_____

_____

_____

_____

_____

_____

_____

_____

_____

_____

_____

_____

_____

_____

_____

_____

_____

_____

My Recipes

My Recipes

My Recipes

My Recipes

My Recipes